BY

PRISM

Uplifting Views on Daily Life

Adapted freely from the teachings of

The Rebbe
Rabbi Menachem Mendel Schneerson

of righteous memory

Compiled and adapted by
Dovid Zaklikowski

MERKOS L'INYONEI CHINUCH

SUITE|302

Contents

Introduction

The Rebbe, Rabbi Menachem Mendel Schneerson, of righteous memory, inspired a generation of men and women to transform Jewish life across the globe. His teachings are studied until this day by followers, admirers and laymen across the globe. What makes the Rebbe's views so unique?

The Rebbe saw this world as a good and holy place. He saw that in essence every human being is decent, and that no person should be disregarded. He viewed any bad traits as merely an outer layer.

This approach stemmed from the Rebbe's ability to look at our universe from above, from a G-dly perspective. The Rebbe understood that, essentially, what G-d created cannot be evil, bad or repulsive. It is good, and all one needs to do is look beneath the veneer. Through this prism the Rebbe guided our generation. Whether through teachings, campaigns or personal advice, he shifted the attitude and focus from mundane to divine.

The Rebbe utilized an endless number of resources to influence and promote goodness in our time, while paying heed to our rich history and tradition. This booklet attempts to illustrate 42 years of the Rebbe's leadership by utilizing his talks and correspondence from each year, in order to give you a sense of the Rebbe's unique and varied approach to all aspects of life.

Through Torah, the Rebbe explained, ancient teachings respond directly to modern issues. For hours at a time the Rebbe elucidated Torah texts, biblical narratives and Jewish traditions, and brilliantly extrapolated lessons that are as relevant to our daily lives as ever. The quotes presented here are adapted from their original sources in Yiddish, Hebrew and English (sources are listed at the end of the booklet). Any errors are on the part of the compiler.

We hope that this booklet will inspire a heightened understanding of the Rebbe's ideals, and encourage introspection and positive change in your life, which will certainly be another step toward the ultimate redemption, with the coming of Moshiach, speedily in our days.

Rebuilding

Though the Rebbe and his wife, Rebbetzin Chaya Mushka, narrowly escaped the German occupation, they lost relatives, possessions, and life as they had known it. In the United States, the sixth Chabad rebbe, Rabbi Yosef Yitzchak Schneersohn, worked tirelessly to save Jews from war-torn Europe, and to rebuild Judaism in the aftermath of the Holocaust. Upon Rabbi Yosef Yitzchak's passing in 1950, the Rebbe continued his legacy. He wrote to Holocaust survivor and Nobel laureate Elie Wiesel:

> It is no doubt an obligation to never forget what our enemies have done to us, but it is no less an obligation to fight the assimilation that is plaguing the Jewish nation. We need to be active in rebuilding our people by bringing Jewish children into the world, promoting Jewish education and teaching by example.

The Rebbe delivers a talk in the early 1950s.

Leadership

Following the passing of the sixth Chabad Rebbe, Rabbi Yosef Yitzchak, the Rebbe refused to accept the official mantle of leadership of the movement, though he continued his involvement with its educational branch. For an entire year, many Chabad disciples beseeched the Rebbe to accept the position. The Rebbe finally conceded after his wife, Rebbetzin Chaya Mushka, daughter of the sixth rebbe, implored her husband to consent, lest her father's work be lost. The Rebbe constantly stressed that every individual needs to be a leader – of him or herself, his or her surroundings and everyone he or she meets. Stressing this in his inaugural talk, the Rebbe stated:

King David could have built the Holy Temple in Jerusalem on his own, yet he chose to involve the entire community. A leader can assist, guide and provide suggestions. However, each individual needs to utilize their own intelligence and drive to fulfill their mission in this world.

Femininity

The Rebbe explained that men and women alike have stakes in Jewish life, despite their different spiritual needs. To augment the role of women in Judaism, the Rebbe encouraged women to accept leadership positions, especially in educational institutions. He also encouraged the establishment of the Lubavitch Women's Organization, which organizes Jewish study groups, outreach events and programming:

It is incumbent upon each person to reach out to all Jews and teach them about Judaism and their Jewish heritage. Women are blessed with an innate sympathetic and tender nature, and therefore it is of great importance for them to be involved in influencing others.

One of the first Chabad women's conventions in the United States.

A group of public school children march outside Lubavitch World Headquarters.

Pride

Following the Holocaust, many Jews limited their religious observance to their own homes and institutions. The Rebbe stated that Judaism needs to be celebrated joyously and openly. One of the Rebbe's first initiatives was a parade celebrating Jewish pride and unity. Until today, children from Jewish day schools and public schools descend on historic Eastern Parkway in Brooklyn with banners promoting Jewish themes and observance. The Nazis, wrote the Rebbe, proved that even European Jews who concealed their Jewish identity were found out. He explained that there is no benefit in hiding one's Judaism; in fact, being proud will compel others to respect you for your religious convictions:

With so many unaffiliated Jews, practicing Judaism openly evokes Jewish pride, a spirit of Jewish identity and way of life. There is no reason to hide one's Jewishness in this free country. Public practice of Judaism is in keeping with the American slogan *"e pluribus unum"* – out of many, one. The American culture has been enriched by the thriving ethnic cultures which contribute, each in its own way, to American life, both materially and spiritually.

Peer Pressure

America gave Jews the ability to express freedom of religion, yet it also encouraged many to replace their Jewish culture with American culture. The Rebbe encouraged Jews to renew their Jewish identity – both in and out of their homes. The Rebbe understood that it can be difficult to grow in Jewish observance when one's neighbor seems lax. He explained that we need to learn positive traits from our neighbors, and discard the negative ones. To a group of Jewish children who wanted to go to public school like their neighborhood friends, he said:

> What did Noah do when building the ark? Did he succumb to peer pressure? What did our forefather Abraham do? Did he listen to his idolatrous visitors? What did the great Jewish leader Moses do? Was he influenced by his Egyptian surroundings? We need to learn from our great Jewish leaders, and not flounder under the pressure of what our neighbors may say.

Obstacles

As Chabad-Lubavitch continued to grow, there became a clear need for a volunteer branch that would organize ongoing activities. Thus the Lubavitch Youth Organization in North America was born. The Rebbe addressed difficulties that might hinder the organization's progress:

Many times, meetings beget more meetings, which beget more meetings. To achieve results, there must be action immediately after the first meeting. Do not fear the possibility of failure, as it is a lesson for the future. The fourth Chabad rebbe, Rabbi Shmuel, said, "The world says that if there is no way to go under, go over. I say that one should leap over from the start." Instead of becoming stagnant due to challenges, disregard them and move forward — joyously — without looking back.

Terror

The people of Israel were living in fear due to Palestinian terrorists who would commit attacks on Jewish communities. In a small village near Tel Aviv, inhabited by many survivors of Soviet and Nazi oppression, terrorists murdered five students and a teacher at the Chabad vocational school. In response, the Rebbe sent a group of students to comfort the Chabad community with a message:

> There is no just explanation – theological or otherwise – for what happened. Silence is key. However, you can be comforted by continuing to build the village and its institutions. This is the appropriate response to tragedy, and not through capitulating to terror.

At work in the rebuilt Chabad vocational school *in Kfar Chabad, Israel.*

Responsibility

The Rebbe believed that every man, woman and child should care about the material and spiritual needs of others, and not only about one's own personal welfare. In the early years of his leadership this concept had yet to be fully incorporated in the communal psyche, and so the Rebbe frequently stressed this concept. On the holiday of Sukkot, the Rebbe related the idea of Jewish unity to the palm branch that we combine with three additional plants – the citrus, myrtle and willow:

Each of the Four Kinds is very different. One has a good smell and taste; one only smells good; one only has a good taste; and one has neither taste nor smell. Our sages explain that these represent different kinds of Jews. There's one kind of Jew that is learned and does good deeds; one kind that only practices good deeds; another kind that is just learned, and one that has neither quality. Just as there is no way to fulfill the Sukkot commandment without all four plant species, no Jew can be left behind. The same way we bring together palm, citrus, myrtle and willow, all Jews need to unite together to fulfill G-d's will.

An Israeli soldier shakes the Four Kinds outside a mobile "Mitzvah Tank" home.

Food

It's an established reality – and sometimes a humorous one – that much of Judaism is celebrated around a holiday table. Additionally, there are numerous laws regarding food. The Kabbalists say, and many would concur, that there is nothing like fulfilling G-d's commandments via traditions that are connected with food. The Rebbe commented:

Before eating bread, we make a blessing to thank G-d for providing nourishment, and we have in mind the positive acts we'll complete with the energy we've gleaned. In Judaism, the spiritual is not disconnected from the material. This concept is expressed best in food which, when eaten for holy purposes, integrates the spiritual into our physical bodies.

Chabad House

The Rebbe unveiled a vision in which Jewish centers would sprout across the globe, with the goal of reaching every Jew regardless of their background. Today these centers are known as Chabad Houses, and number in the thousands. The Rebbe described their mission statement:

> They should be centers that spread goodness and kindness as embodied in Jewish teachings. The spirit of the center should be permeated with chassidic light, vitality and warmth, based on the three loves – the love of G-d, the love of the Torah; and the love of our people, Israel – which are ultimately one entity.

A live radio show from Lubavitch World Headquarters.

Technology

The 20th century was marked by a wave of new technology that brought the world directly into one's home. The state of the art morphed from telephone, to radio, to television and the Internet. Chabad utilized these advances in technology to enhance the lives of Jews who might not participate in Jewish life otherwise. The Rebbe explained:

Everything that G-d created is potentially good. Certainly, technology that allows a person to be heard at the other end of the world has the potential to be utilized for the good. It is our free choice to use technology for its intended purpose to spread goodness and holiness or, G-d forbid, the opposite.

Song

Chabad teachings places great emphasis on music, and contains a large repertoire of compositions. The Rebbe himself taught 13 melodies, most of them Chabad songs that had been forgotten, or melodies he heard from chassidic luminaries. In 1961, the Rebbe taught the melody *Anim Zemiros*, a powerful soul-stirring melody to the Hebrew words "I sing hymns and compose songs because my soul longs for You. My soul desires Your shelter, to know all Your ways." The Rebbe related that he learned this melody years earlier, when someone still engrossed in the aura of Yom Kippur continued singing it hours after the holiday had ended. On the power of song, the Rebbe explained:

Melody is the quill of the soul. Words may be an expression of your heart, but a melody expresses the contents of your soul. A good melody not only expresses the soul, but it is like a quill in hand: it brings one to action.

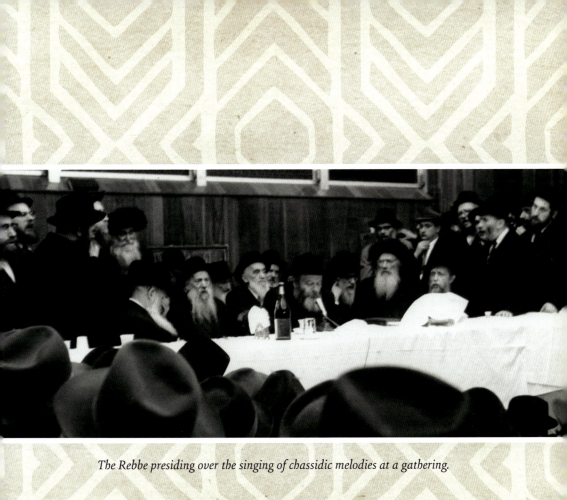

The Rebbe presiding over the singing of chassidic melodies at a gathering.

Conflict

While we may never agree with someone else's way of life, the Rebbe taught that this does not need to impinge on your friendship. The Rebbe, who championed unconditional acceptance of all Jews, concurrently explained that one does not need to lower their standards of Jewish practice in order to reach their friends. In a long correspondence with the acclaimed sculptor Jacques Lipchitz regarding a specific area of Jewish law, the Rebbe explained his approach:

> I am not G–d's policeman. Yet I consider it my duty to influence a Jew from doing something which, in my opinion, is not recommended. On the other hand, it is my policy to seek out points of agreement rather than disagreement. Since we have reached an impasse in our discussion, I prefer to turn my attention to points of mutual agreement.

Harmony

Rabbi Schneur Zalman, founder of Chabad, upheld a philosophy that inspires trust in G-d, morality, and a deep responsibility to promote all that is vital for a wholesome human society. The Rebbe explained:

> Judaism places emphasis on action. Thus, the purpose of knowledge is to ultimately translate it into deed. Chabad philosophy goes a step further. It explains that each act contains a soul. A person can achieve true harmony by elevating an action, thereby revealing its intrinsic soul. This harmony is reflected in the spiritual, emotional and physical facets by revealing our divine souls, uplifting our physical bodies, and promoting harmony with the world we live in.

The Rebbe with his mother (sitting, center) in 1947 in Paris, France.

Parents

Rabbi Levi Yitzchak Schneerson, father of the Rebbe, was exiled to a remote location in the Soviet Union as punishment for his efforts on behalf of the Jewish community. He passed away in 1944. The Rebbe's mother, Rebbetzin Chana, arrived in the United States in 1947. The Rebbe's respect for his parents was boundless. Following her arrival in the United States, the Rebbe would visit his mother daily. He was careful to never turn his back to her. In 1964, in commemoration of the 20th anniversary of his father's passing, the Rebbe began an initiative to establish an interest-free loan society for Jewish schools and parents. Regarding the commandment to honor one's parents, the Rebbe explained:

> It is a logical principle to respect those who gave us life and sustenance from an early age. However, there is another dimension to honoring our parents, and it is that G-d is also a partner in our creation. G-d commands us to honor our parents, and thus we honor G-d, too.

Teaching

When the Rebbe's mother , Reb- betzin Chana, passed away, he chose to memorialize her by delivering scholarly talks on the biblical commentator Rabbi Shlomo Yitzchaki, known as Rashi. The Rebbe's talks fill over 200 volumes; a large percentage of them are in-depth analyses of the commentary, which the Rebbe elucidated based on specific rules and guidelines. According to Rashi, his commentary is intended to be accessible to a child, yet it contains multiple dimensions that scholars have been exploring since its original publication:

Rabbi Shlomo Yitzchaki was a great scholar and authority on Jewish law. He was a famed teacher who educated some of the top Talmudic scholars. Rashi's prized commentary, however, was meant to be understandable to even the youngest of children. This is the sign of a great leader: despite his tremendous scholarship, he cared for the smallest child.

Darkness

The Rebbe transformed everything he heard, saw or read into a lesson. The Rebbe related one story in which two friends enter a dim basement, in the days prior to air conditioning, to cool off. One tells the other, "Don't worry about the dark; soon it will be bright." The other fellow responds, "You are mistaken. It will always be dark, but you'll just become accustomed to the dark."

When we know that it is dark and we are low on spiritual fuel, we can always make changes for the better. Knowing what is wrong is already half the cure. However, when you think that the dark is actually light, and you've become accustomed to the dark, then it is in fact truly dark; such a soul is in need of a recharge.

Mitzvah

When Israel was on the verge of war in 1967, the Rebbe called on all Jews to increase their Jewish observance, specifically encouraging men to don *Tefillin*, encased ritual parchments worn on the arm and head. The Rebbe inspired his followers to go out onto the streets to find Jews to lay Tefillin. Many did so for the first time. The Rebbe emphasized that every single Jew, no matter his or her current situation, needs to be reached, and that even a single positive act is important:

> Every mitzvah, good deed, is everlasting and connects you with the divine. The sages state that every person, even a wicked one, is filled with mitzvahs. Thus, each deed — and the connection it creates with G-d — is an eternal bond that can never be severed, despite a person's standing.

Donning tefillin on the streets of New York City during the Six-Day War.

Conversation with a Jewish inmate.

Prison

It can be easy to forget those behind bars. Sometimes their actions are abhorrent and have brought harm to many people. However, the Rebbe felt strongly that this segment of society should not be neglected, and encouraged outreach toward Jewish inmates. Years later, he explained his reasoning to Israeli Prime Minister Yitzhak Rabin:

> The purpose of prison should not be to simply punish or pain the imprisoned. In prison, the jailed person should become a free man — not physically — but mentally and spiritually. He should arrive at a place in which he regrets the past, corrects his ways and establishes his future in a just life that is free of crime and wrongdoing.

Neighbors

In the 1960s, many neighborhoods across the United States began to deteriorate. Affluent areas that once had prospered became slums, dangerous to inhabit. With each person who moved, neighborhoods continued to change dramatically. Their actions detrimentally affected local real estate, stores, synagogues, charities, the elderly and religious organizations. The Rebbe beseeched:

Think not of yourself, but of your neighbors. Ask, "What damage will I be causing them? How will my actions affect their situation? What will happen to those who can't afford to move? To the many who haven't the strength to begin life anew?" Our sages said, "Don't do to others what you don't want done to you."

Livelihood

Maimonides wrote that the greatest form of charity is to find someone a livelihood. The Rebbe constantly sought creative ways to find and provide people with opportunities to earn an income, from commissioning an artist to produce work for a publication to connecting a jeweler with a group of Holocaust survivors to whom he taught jewelry-making. Yet the Rebbe strongly affirmed that while one must be proactive in finding a livelihood, one's income, business or job should not consume the entire day:

You may be running to pursue a livelihood, but in reality you may be running away from it, for it is chasing you. Do not allow your day to be consumed by work while disregarding the other dimensions of your life — namely, family and spirituality. Wherever you are, you have to create a vessel, and G-d will provide for you.

Soviet Jewry

The Chabad movement wasn't welcome in the Soviet Union. Many Chabad activists, including the sixth Chabad rebbe, Rabbi Yosef Yitzchak Schneerson, were jailed and expelled from the country. As Jews worldwide protested the fate of Russian Jewry, Chabad's clandestine network continued to operate. The Rebbe maintained secret communication with his followers in the country, and sent emissaries posing as tourists to teach and deliver ritual items. Living in constant danger, one 17-year-old wrote to the Rebbe. He did not ask about material needs, or his fears regarding the future; instead, he wrote to the Rebbe that he has difficulty concentrating during prayer, and asked for advice. The Rebbe repeated the story to his followers, along with this message:

A clandestine prayer service in the Soviet Union.

Let's learn about our priorities. We live in a free and democratic country. We have an abundance of material good, and we practice our religion freely. Yet we complain that we do not have enough livelihood. There are Jews who live behind the Iron Curtain in poverty, yet they are not concerned with material needs. Every Jewish observance is an act of great self-sacrifice. They save potatoes for Passover so they will have what to eat. They worry all week about how they will miss school and work on Shabbat and Jewish holidays without getting into trouble with the authorities. This is the contrast we need to make when calculating our material assets.

Retirement

For many, the act of retirement is reverent, and has become a rite of passage. Shifting from a life of constant productivity to one of respite is the norm. Prior to his 70th birthday, the Rebbe received a barrage of letters advising him to relax in his duties. The Rebbe suggested that instead of being less productive, Chabad should develop an additional 71 institutions:

> G-d told Adam: "You are here to care and toil for My world." When G-d created the world, He formed it in a way that requires us to work for our physical and spiritual needs. The act of receiving without effort is displeasing in the eyes of the Torah, since we become partners with G-d when we toil toward goodness. This should not change – as much as is physically possible – even as one becomes older.

The Rebbe presides over the gathering in honor of his 70th birthday.

Books

As we beautify our homes and attempt to create a space that reflects our values and personalities, we can lose sight of what truly counts. The Rebbe called on people to invest in "spiritual furniture" – holy books and Jewish educational texts – to adorn the home. While we try to keep physical furniture in good condition, books should be used well:

> Time should never be wasted. Time ought to be used to gain knowledge. Having Jewish books in your library will always give you an opportunity – whether you wake during the night, or have a few minutes by day – to maximize your time to the fullest.

Charity

Judaism sees charity not simply as a favor for another, but as a charitable act toward ourselves. The Hebrew word for charity, *tzedakah*, stems from the word *tzedek*, which means justice, implying that it is a just act to give. The Rebbe established a charity campaign that encouraged distribution of coins at events, so that people would have the opportunity to give charity. The Rebbe advised that charity boxes contain a disclaimer that the owner may give the full charity box to a cause of his or her choosing, stressing that the benefit of charity lies in the act, and not the specific recipient:

G-d grants you money as collateral, since He trusts that you will use it wisely. When you give charity to one in need, to someone whom you owe nothing, and give more than you think affordable, G-d — who owes you nothing — will increase His charity toward you, and give you with an open hand.

Women

The Rebbe understood that women provide a stable foundation for the home. Jewish life, in fact, centers on the home, not the synagogue. Home is a safe haven, a place to which we return at the end of the day, and it is where the lives of our children are shaped. Women are seminal to Jewish life and childrearing, and therefore have unique observances:

Women and girls light the Shabbat and holiday candles, which bring peace and warmth into the home. The lights of Shabbat also bring inspiration to our daily lives by illuminating our week, and help us navigate our struggles. The light shows us that, in essence, the world is good and can be used for spiritual purposes. It is the woman of the home who creates this light.

Assistance

Synagogues are commonly understood to be places of prayer, communal study and reflection. The Rebbe encouraged constant growth in these areas, but also suggested that synagogues become reservoirs of kindness with the establishment of interest-free loan societies. A loan is a special form of charity, as it allows a person to overcome a hardship without feeling ashamed that they are receiving a handout. The Rebbe also called on children to establish interest-free loan societies in their classrooms:

Every class should establish an interest-free loan society. The children should donate and contribute their time to the society. The class should elect a president, treasurer and officers. Elections should happen often, and all the students should have the opportunity to be elected over the course of a school year. This will give the children a sense of responsibility towards the community, and will teach them to do kindness from a young age.

Intellect

Many Chabad teachings weren't published until the middle of the 20th century, when the Rebbe led the publication division of the movement prior to his predecessor's passing in 1950. In 1977, the Rebbe decided to print *Ayin-Beit*, the monumental and expansive work of Rabbi Sholom DovBer, the fifth Chabad rebbe, known as the Rebbe Rashab. Chabad philosophy – as depicted in this unique work – delves into all aspects of Jewish scholarship, spanning creation, the world's constitution, purpose, the human psyche and faith. The volumes of Chassidus provide a multifaceted approach to serving G-d:

To serve G-d with emotions or with faith is not enough. This would be an incomplete service. There must be a fusion of these elements. Intellect is the ruler of faith and emotions. One must use his or her intellect, and not be content with a service of G-d that centers only on emotions or faith exclusive of the other.

Vice President Walter Mondale addresses the event marking Education Day U.S.A.

Education

In 1978, President Jimmy Carter inaugurated Education Day U.S.A., in tribute to the Rebbe's efforts on behalf of education. This day, marked on the Rebbe's Jewish birthday, was celebrated with great fanfare in the Capitol, and is still marked yearly with a presidential proclamation. In a letter to Vice-President Walter F. Mondale, the Rebbe explained his philosophy of education:

> Education should not be limited to the acquisition of knowledge and preparation for a career. Education should teach a child how to live a better life, not only for the individual, but for the advancement of society as a whole. Therefore, the educational system must pay more attention — indeed, this must be its central focus — to the building of character, with emphasis on moral and ethical values.

Differences

When two Chabad students visited Iran in 1979, they planned to lay grounds for the opening of a Chabad House. Instead, the revolution that ripped through the country led them to spearhead an operation that saved thousands of Jewish children. Just as the revolution was coming to a head, they orchestrated a daring escape in which children were airlifted to Italy, and later brought to the United States. Chabad communities cared for their physical needs and encouraged them to maintain their unique Persian observances. Chabad helped establish the Persian Jewish Center of Brooklyn, a synagogue and learning center for Iranian families. To the South African Jewish Board of Deputies, the Rebbe expressed his appreciation for every community's unique traditions and the importance of preserving them:

A class of Iranian immigrants study in a school run by Chabad.

∽ 54 ∾

Virtually every Jewish community comprises a variety of groups, each with a distinct identity in terms of ancestral heritage and traditions, as exemplified by different synagogues with different customs, such as Ashkenaz, Sephardic, Yemenite, etc. Side-by-side, they contribute to the advancement of the Jewish community as a whole. You surely know that the rabbis in all generations scrupulously upheld the validity of tradition in regard to the various canons of prayer services, tracing its variety to the original Twelve Tribes of Israel. Experience has shown that whenever a uniform educational system has been imposed on a multi-faceted community, it inevitably proved disastrous.

Elderly

The Rebbe felt that retirees should never truly retire, but continue to remain intellectually active and honest. He encouraged the establishment of learning circles for retired men and women to study Jewish scholarly texts. The Rebbe requested that groups have a set schedule, designated place and study track. He said that bringing retirees together to learn will heighten the recognition that, indeed, they are the most integral part of the family unit:

Referring to someone as an "elder" should not be derogatory; it should indicate an advanced stage of understanding and knowledge. Asking them for advice is not for their own good − it is for yours. Their wisdom can alleviate many doubts and discord, and prevent mistakes that one can make in life.

1981

Children

The Rebbe felt that directly combating the irreverence of today's youth would be a futile effort. He instead established a Jewish club that would encourage children to willingly join a "spiritual army" that encourages acts of goodness, and motivates a child to strengthen his or her Jewish observance:

The club utilizes contests, gatherings and awards, and is designed as a hierarchy — as all armies are — in which a child graduates to higher rankings the more "missions" he completes. This instills a sense of authority, and the notion that children must respect their parents, teachers, elders and the Commander-in-Chief, G-d Almighty.

Unity

A year after calling upon Jewish children to unite toward the writing of a Torah scroll, the Rebbe led a movement to inspire all Jews to take part in the writing of Torah scrolls. During that year, many new Torah scrolls were written across the globe. The Rebbe explained why this act of unity is so unique:

> We must love our neighbors as we do ourselves, while appreciating our diversity. Every community has unique traditions, yet every person is an individual. The Torah scroll contains many different letters, corresponding to the diversity within our nation. When people come together in the writing of a Torah – each taking a financial stake – the intrinsic value of our extended family is expressed via G-d's timeless words and teachings. It exemplifies what our sages say: G-d, the Torah and the Jewish nation are all one.

The completion of the first children's Torah scroll at the Western Wall in Jerusalem.

Morality

A child may feel that, in the absence of constant surveillance, they can do as they please. Therefore, the Rebbe felt that children need to be taught that there is a higher Being who sees all. He wanted this to be included in the public-school curriculum, but laws regarding separation of church and state prohibited the teaching of anything related to G-d within school walls. Instead, the Rebbe encouraged instituting a moment of silence:

> At the start of the school day, students should take a moment of silence. They should be guided to contemplate on what is important to them. They will then question their parents, "What is most important? What should I be thinking about?" The parent will explain their beliefs, their faith in a Creator and the fact that He is constantly watching over us. This will create tangible changes in our children, our families and our society.

Maimonides

The Rebbe encouraged people to participate in daily study of Maimonides' work on Jewish law, the *Mishneh Torah*. The fourteen volumes of *Mishneh Torah* contain a digest of all Jewish laws, including those that will be applicable only during the messianic era. The Rebbe suggested several tracks of learning based on time availability, and even one for young children. In one talk, the Rebbe examined the way Maimonides opens his volumes, and provided a commentary on utilizing our talents:

Maimonides chose to begin his magnum opus with "In the name of the L-rd, the everlasting G-d" (Genesis 21:33). Although his volume is replete with brilliant scholarship, Maimonides expresses a firm belief that his talents were granted to him by G-d. He then adds the verse "Then shall I not be ashamed, when I have regard for all of Your commandments" (Psalms 119:6). How did Maimonides have the boldness to chronicle the entire corpus of Jewish law? Maimonides understood, as he explained in his opening, that when you are on the right path, and G-d graces you with a talent, you cannot ignore it. If one avoids utilizing their talents, this is not called modesty; rather, it is listening to your animalistic inclination to shy away from your calling in the world.

Justice

Jews have lived under many an oppressive regime, which often prevented the promulgation of the Seven Noahide Laws. These laws are moral biblical directives from G-d, given prior to the creation of the Jewish nation. In 1985, the Rebbe began a campaign to promote these laws to the masses. He believed that today, when we all have dealings with the world – when most of the world adheres to the rules of kindness and justice, and most live in freedom – we should teach these basic tenets widely:

In our time, a nation that trumpeted human rights, and even animal rights, chose to perpetrate some of the cruelest acts humanity has ever seen. If they would have recognized that G-d was watching them, a G-d who commanded them to not murder or steal, the Holocaust would have not been possible to such an extent.

Mentor

Central to the teachings of Chassidism is the idea of learning from all that happens around us, including those we meet. The Rebbe took this a step further, based on the teaching in Ethics of Our Fathers to "appoint for yourself a master." The Rebbe encouraged every person to find a confidant to whom he could speak with about life issues, or any pressing matters:

> A person is too close to his or her own self. When in doubt, a person cannot fully rely on their intellect to make the best objective decision. Asking another person — someone who has no personal bias — will clear any doubt. Speaking to your mentor from time to time about where you stand spiritually will give you a non-biased opinion on areas that can be improved.

Joy

Joy is critical to a healthy and balanced life. Chabad leaders stressed that an integral part of being content and joyous is recognizing that every-thing ultimately stems from goodness, even when it isn't apparent. The Rebbe said:

> You would likely be joyous if the president of the United States chose you for a position. G–d placed His lofty spiritual worlds to the side, and said that they were all created for the sake of our world. Thus, you should be joyous, for the King of all kings has chosen you over another spiritual being to be His envoy and to fulfill His tenets.

Birthdays

Rebbetzin Chaya Mushka Schneerson, wife of the Rebbe, led a very private life. Few ever met her, and most were unaware of the tremendous support she provided the Rebbe. At her funeral, the Rebbe's raw emotions were palpable. Despite his pain, the Rebbe encouraged others to take to heart his wife's good deeds and to create initiatives in her memory. A month after her passing, on her birthday, the Rebbe began a mass campaign to publicly celebrate one's Jewish birthday in a meaningful manner that stressed Jewish study, charity, a gathering with friends and positive resolutions:

Every breath we take, and everything that happens around us, is miraculous. Yet we do not contemplate this idea every moment of every day. On our birthdays, however, we take the time to specifically acknowledge the miraculous events around us, as we mark the miracle of our birth. On this day we reflect on the purity with which we came into this world, and we are given the extra ability to return to our pure and wholesome roots.

Dignitaries come to wish the Rebbe a happy birthday at a gathering to mark the occasion.

Childhood

A child, the Rebbe expressed, is like a sapling in need of attention. A sapling must be regularly watered, cared for and watched over until it becomes a strong and beautiful tree. The child also requires attention, love and care so that he or she can grow into a healthy human being. The Rebbe explained the importance of a good education:

There are two ways to heal a patient. The first is to wait for him or her to become sick, and then address the illness. The second is to practice preventative medicine, and ensure that the person does not become sick. Crime is part of reality; but by restructuring the education system to recognize the roots of malice, we can better educate our children and avoid crime preemptively.

Purpose

One of the mission statements of Chabad philosophy is to create a fitting place for G-d in this world. This is based on a statement by our sages, "G-d desired to have a dwelling place here below." The Rebbe explained:

In this material world, G-d wants us to utilize our skills toward fulfilling His will. There is another dimension of service that is above our understanding, which is G-d's unexplainable desire for this world to be holy. This, too, G-d wants us to express by serving Him in a way that is beyond our comprehension. Ultimately, we strive toward blending both kinds of service. This is done by fulfilling G-d's will while allowing His infinite light to penetrate our very being, until we are capable of seeing this light in our every action.

A Chabad "roving rabbi" in Namibia during a light moment with locals.

Anti-Semitism

In 1991, Saddam Hussein, in a murderous act, fired Scud missiles into the heart of Israel. Around the world, anti-Semitic acts were on the rise, including riots in the Crown Heights community in Brooklyn, New York. In Poland, too, the Jewish community was on alert. The Rebbe, in a letter to the Council for Polish-Jewish Relations, explained:

Mankind began with a single individual: Adam. G-d designed the human race this way so that every person would know that we descend from the same individual, who was created in the image of G-d. As such, no human being can claim to be of superior ancestral origin, and we can easily cultivate feelings of kinship in all interpersonal relationships.

Future

Judaism views this world as a springboard to a better and more refined world. The messianic dream of Jews for thousands of years is of a world where G-dliness prevails openly, and His presence is revealed. We will understand that what we view now as challenging and dark is, in fact, ultimate good. Our goal in this world is to reveal the underlying goodness. The Rebbe recognized that our changing world was moving toward a better time, where peace is preferred over bloodshed, where world powers and individuals combat poverty and starvation. Through positive actions, the Rebbe said, we bring the redemption closer. The Rebbe explained how we can best prepare for the messianic era:

The world was created for you. You have the ability to change the world via your mission in this world. Just as each person has a specific purpose, skillset or career, so too, each moment has a specific mission. You may think, "What am I doing here now? Could I not be doing better elsewhere?" You have to focus on where you are now, not about where you could be. You have to strive to bring completion and holiness into your immediate surroundings.

Sources

Adapted freely from the teachings and talks of the Lubavitcher Rebbe.

Below are the sources (note that several of the quotes are not published in book format and are therefore not sourced to any specific volume):

Page 8 Igros Kodesh, vol. 23, p. 374. • p. 11 Toras Menachem vol. 2, p. 213; Sichos Kodesh 5731, vol. 1, p. 336ff. • p. 12 Toras Menachem, vol. 7, p. 116ff; Igros Kodesh, vol. 5, p. 8; Toras Menachem, vol. 9, p. 108. • p. 15 Toras Menachem, vol. 8, p. 148; letter, Teves 3, 5742. • p. 16 Toras Menachem, vol. 12, p. 190. • p. 17 Toras Menachem, vol. 14, p. 64; Toras Menachem 5746, vol. 1, p. 145. • p. 18 Likkutei Sichos, vol. 12, p. 258; Igros Kodesh, vol. 13, p. 239. • p. 20 Toras Menachem, vol. 18, pp. 31ff. • p. 22 Toras Menachem, vol. 23, pp. 84ff. • p. 23 Igros Kodesh, vol. 18, p. 499; letter, Adar 19, 5729. • p. 25 Toras Menachem 5744, vol. 2, pp. 1040ff. • p. 26 Toras Menachem, vol. 18, p. 30; Toras Menachem, vol. 32, p. 112; Toras Menachem 5747, vol. 1, p. 92. • p. 28 Letter, Erev Pesach, 5722; Sichos Kodesh, Kedoshim 5727, p. 107. • p. 29 Letter, Teves 20, 5744; the Rebbe's foreword to Rabbi Shneur Zalman of Liadi: Biography, p. IX. • p. 31 Sefer Haminhagim, p. 100; Likkutei Sichos, vol. 36, p. 95. • p. 32 Likkutei Sichos, vol. 5, p. 279; Sichos Kodesh 5736, vol. 2, p. 715. • p. 33 Sichos Kodesh 5736, p. 281. • p. 34 Sichos Kodesh 5727, p. 122; Toras Menachem 5743, vol. 3, p. 1210; Likkutei Sichos, vol. 5, p. 91. • p. 37 Letter, Erev Pesach, 5736. • p. 38 Sichos Kodesh 5729, pp. 68–9. • p. 39 Sichos Kodesh 5731, p. 73. • p. 40 Sichos Kodesh 5728, vol. 1, p. 96; Toras Menachem 5742, vol. 3, p. 1351. • p. 42 Sichos Kodesh 5732, pp. 99ff. • p. 44 Sichos Kodesh 5733, p. 201. • p. 45 Igros Kodesh, vol. 29, p. 11; Likkutei Sichos, vol. 2, p. 410. • p. 47 Likkutei Sichos, vol. 17, p. 146; Toras Menachem 5750, vol. 3, p. 345. • p. 48 Likkutei Sichos, vol. 14, p. 374; Likkutei Sichos, vol. 16, p. 625. • p. 50 Interview with the Rebbe, March 7, 1960. • p. 53 Letter, February 26, 1979. • p. 54 Letter, 1980. • p. 56 Sichos Kodesh 5740, pp. 883ff; ibid., pp. 972ff. • p. 59 Sichos Kodesh 5741, pp. 177ff; letter, Teves 26, 5742. • p. 60 Sichos Kodesh 5741, vol. 4, p. 764; Likkutei Sichos, vol. 24, p. 583. • p. 62 Toras Menachem 5743, vol. 3, p. 1298; Toras Menachem 5746, pp. 405ff. • p. 63 Toras Menachem 5744, vol. 3, p. 1546; ibid, pp. 1605ff. • p. 64 Toras Menachem, vol. 5, p. 2722; letter, Erev Shabbos Bereishis, 5747. • p. 66 Toras Menachem 5746, vol. 4, pp. 173ff. • p. 67 Toras Menachem 5747, vol. 4, p. 421; letter, 5736. • p. 68 Toras Menachem 5748, vol. 3, p. 158; Toras Menachem, vol. 33, pp. 283ff. • p. 70 Sefer Hasichos 5749, vol. 1, p. 28; talk of April 15, 1981. • p. 72 Toras Menachem 5750, vol. 2, pp. 312ff. • p. 74 Letter, Cheshvan 15, 5752. • p. 76 Talk of Shabbos Mishpatim, 5752; talk of Shabbos Pinchas, 5751 (Shaarei Geulah, pp. 170ff).